N ᴄ S

# CHRISTIANITY

In this book, CE stands for
Common Era and BCE for
Before Common Era, with the
Common Era beginning in the year 0

The publishers would like to thank the following editorial
consultants for their help:
Dr Sue Hamilton, Department of Theology and
Religious Studies, King's College, London
The Reverend Leslie Houlden, formerly Professor of New
Testament Studies, King's College, London
Keith Ward, Regius Professor of Divinity Emeritus,
University of Oxford

KINGFISHER

Kingfisher Publications Plc
New Penderel House, 283-288 High Holborn, London WC1V 7HZ

First published as *The Kingfisher Book of Religions* by Kingfisher Publications Plc 1999
Revised and updated edition published by Kingfisher Publications Plc 2005

2 4 6 8 10 9 7 5 3 1

1TR/0405/SHENS/MA(MA)/158MA

A CIP catalogue record for this book is available from the British Library

ISBN 13: 0-978-7534-1104-9
ISBN 10: 0-7534-1104-0

Colour separations by Modern Age
Printed in Taiwan

WORLD FAITHS

# CHRISTIANITY

Worship, festivals and ceremonies from around the world

TREVOR BARNES

KINGFISHER

# CONTENTS

# INTRODUCTION

The founder of Christianity was a Jew named Jesus, a teacher and healer who lived some 2,000 years ago in Palestine. His life, death and resurrection became the basis for a religion practised by almost a third of the world's population.

### Early ministry

The details of Jesus' life and ministry are found in the four Gospels of what Christians call the New Testament of the Bible. They accept the authority of the Hebrew Bible (for them, the Old Testament), but believe it was superseded by a new covenant with God, of which Jesus was the living sign. Jesus himself said he had not come to alter the scriptures, but to fulfil them. He taught by example, living a simple and selfless life based on love. Christian love has two elements – love of God and love of other people. Despite the cruelty sometimes committed in the name of Christianity, this is the basis of the faith.

*Below Jesus chose 12 apostles, or disciples, to help him spread the word of God (the gospel or 'good news'). They believed him to be the Messiah ('anointed one') foretold in the Hebrew scriptures. On the night before his death, Jesus ate a final meal with his disciples – 'the Last Supper'.*

## 'I and my Father are one.'

John 10:30

### Life and death

In his day, Jesus' teaching was controversial and brought him into conflict not only with the Romans occupying the country but also with the Jewish religious leaders. They considered him to be a false messiah who refused to accept the rulings of the religious authorities – an offence for which the penalty could be death. Jesus was thought to be a threat to the stability of the state, so he was handed over to the Romans and crucified – a death that involved nailing him to a cross and leaving him there to die.

*Above* *The Eucharist, also known as Holy Communion, commemorates the Last Supper and is central to Christian worship.*

*Below* *From its origins in the Mediterranean, Christianity has spread all over the world. Here, Christians remember events leading up to Jesus' resurrection at the Festival of Holy Week in Peru.*

### Resurrection and salvation

The circumstances surrounding Jesus' death are of as much importance as his ministry. The Bible says that, three days after his crucifixion, Jesus rose from the dead and appeared again to his disciples. This miraculous resurrection was taken as proof that he was indeed the Son of God and that his message of salvation was true.

### Spreading the word

Christianity has always been a missionary religion that aims to convert people to its way of life and its message. During the last 2,000 years missionary movements have spread it all over the world. One of the principal figures responsible for spreading Christianity after Christ's death was Paul of Tarsus, a Jew and a Roman citizen who converted to Christianity after seeing a blinding flash of light on the road to Damascus. While some members of this newly formed sect saw Christianity as another branch of Judaism to be reserved for Jews only, Paul argued that it was a universal religion that should be taken to every corner of the world and freely offered to humankind.

# THE DEVELOPMENT OF CHRISTIANITY

From its origins as a simple community of a few disciples who owned few possessions and shared everything, Christianity has become a global religion of great complexity. The Church owns land, buildings, churches, cathedrals and even television stations and satellites to further the Kingdom of God on Earth.

### The Holy Spirit descends

The initial impulse to take the Gospel to every part of the world came at Pentecost and is described in the second chapter of the Acts of the Apostles. The disciples were sitting together deciding how best to spread God's word now that Jesus was no longer with them when suddenly the room was filled with 'a rushing mighty wind and cloven tongues of fire'. They were filled with the Holy Spirit, which enabled them to speak in other languages, and which prompted them to spread the faith far and wide.

### The Holy Roman Empire

In his epistles (letters) Paul describes the community life of the early Christians, who were a minority religion persecuted by the Roman Empire. It was not until Emperor Constantine converted and made Christianity the state religion that their fortunes improved. However, official recognition was a mixed blessing because it became associated with powerful empires that used force to expand their territory.

*Above* Between 46CE and 62CE, Paul travelled around the Mediterranean on missionary journeys. The black line shows his first journey (46–48CE), the green line his second journey (49–52CE) and the red line his third journey (53–57CE). The blue line shows how Paul's fourth journey (59–62CE) took him as far as Rome.

*Below* Peter the Hermit, riding on a donkey, addresses Crusaders on their way to recapture the Holy Land from Islamic occupation in 1096CE.

*Right In the Orthodox tradition, icons, or devotional pictures of holy figures – here Mary and the baby Jesus – are important in worship. Some Western Catholics in the 11th century (and even some Christians today) viewed them with great suspicion, comparing their use to idol worship. This was one of the factors leading to the great split.*

## Division and dissent

As Christianity grew, so too did its divisions. The first major split was the 'Great Schism' of 1054, which resulted in a division between the Western Catholic Church based in Rome and the Eastern Orthodox Church based in Constantinople (now Istanbul in Turkey). Fifty years later, a series of religious and military expeditions known as the Crusades was mounted. These were organized by Christian forces in an attempt to conquer the Holy Land and liberate the holy sites from Muslim control.

Although the Middle Ages, which lasted until the 15th century CE, produced magnificent Christian art and architecture, there was deep unrest. Abuse of religious power, immoral behaviour by priests, bishops and popes and a general neglect of the essentials of the Christian faith were common. Reform was needed.

## Change and reform

The most important of the reforming groups was led by the German theologian Martin Luther (1483–1546), who opposed the Church's sale of 'indulgences'. These were 'pardons', which were handed over by the priests in exchange for cash. They were supposed to release people from their sins and so allow them to buy their way into heaven. Luther condemned this practice and went further still. He stressed 'justification by faith' and argued that no number of good deeds would save people from sin. Forgiveness came only through faith in Jesus. The Lutheran group and other similar movements are known collectively as the Reformation. They upset the power structures of the Western church and split it in two – the Roman Catholic Church, and the breakaway Protestant Church, which itself divided into many different denominations.

*Below The medieval cathedrals are monuments to the intensity of Christian faith in the Middle Ages. This picture, by a French artist of the 15th century, shows the building of a cathedral.*

# THE LIFE OF JESUS

Despite the many divisions within Christianity, all believers try to live a life based on that of their founder, Jesus Christ. Accounts of the life of Jesus Christ were passed on by word of mouth and it was not until some 35 years after his death that they were first written down in story form. The first account was in Mark's Gospel, on which the gospels of Matthew and Luke were partly based. These, known as the Synoptic Gospels (accounts describing Christ's ministry from the same general point of view), were joined by a fourth, John's Gospel, which is different in tone and concentrates less on the life than on the interpretation of the message.

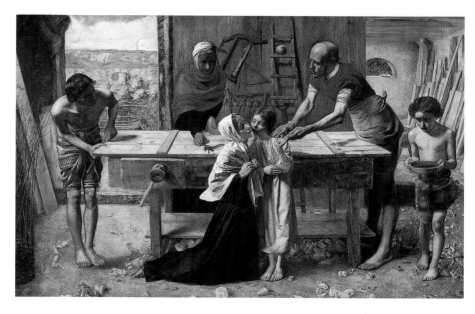

*Above* Christ in the House of His Parents, *painted in 1849–1850 by Sir John Everett Millais, depicts the boyhood of Jesus as a carpenter's son.*

## The life of Christ

The Gospels say that Jesus was born of the Virgin Mary, who conceived him through the power of the Holy Spirit. He was born in Bethlehem and brought up by Mary and her husband Joseph, a carpenter, in Nazareth. When Jesus was about 30 years old his ministry began with his baptism by John the Baptist at the River Jordan. After this he went into the desert to fast and prepare himself spiritually for the work ahead. After 40 days in the wilderness he was tempted by the devil, but resisted. His ministry lasted only three years, but in that time he became a charismatic teacher and healer, impressing people with his goodness, gentleness and strength. Jesus was tolerant of people's failings and slow to condemn.

*Left* In this painting by Piero Della Francesca (c.1419–1492) John the Baptist baptizes Christ at the start of his ministry. The dove is the traditional sign of the Holy Spirit.

*Above* One of Jesus' most famous miracles was the feeding of the 5,000 (Matthew 14:13–21). A crowd of people had come to hear Jesus preach and were amply fed with only five loaves and two fishes.

'I am the door; by me, if any man enter in he shall be saved.'

John 10:9

## Performing miracles

The Bible says that Jesus performed many miracles, such as turning water into wine at the wedding feast at Cana (John 2:1–11). Miracles are not magic tricks done to impress an audience – in Christian thinking they are spiritual signs that show a truth about God's kingdom. The wine is a symbol of the abundance of life that believers in Christ receive.

## A friend to all

Jesus was frequently seen in the company of people rejected by society. In particular he healed lepers, who were considered unclean by the Temple priests. Jesus appealed very much to ordinary people because he spoke in a way they could easily understand. His method was to use parables, that is to say, simple stories to illustrate profound spiritual truths. Among the most famous are the parables of the Good Samaritan, the Unjust Judge, the Great Feast, and the Labourers in the Vineyard. All this was a direct challenge to the Temple authorities, who began to consider how they could get rid of him. One of the last things Jesus did before his arrest was to eat a meal with his disciples. At the Last Supper, Jesus took bread and blessed it, saying, 'This is my body'. In the same way, he took a cup of wine and said to his disciples, 'Drink this in remembrance of me'. The Gospel of Matthew ends with Jesus' promise, 'I am with you always even unto the end of the world'.

11

# THE MINISTRY OF JESUS

**M**ost of what we know of Jesus' earthly ministry comes from the four Gospels of the New Testament. His ministry lasted for not much longer than three years but in that time he changed the course of human history and had a profound effect on the world's understanding of God.

## Jesus' development

We first meet Jesus as a new-born baby (described in Matthew and Luke) and read nothing of his childhood until 12 years later when he reappears in Luke's Gospel as an exceptional boy with amazing gifts that mark him out as someone special. In one passage he is shown arguing and debating with teachers in Jerusalem's Temple and impressing them all with his understanding of religious law. After this, the Gospels fall silent until we meet Jesus again, at around the age of 30, when his adult ministry is about to begin.

*Above* The gently rolling hills above Galilee on the shores of Lake Tiberias were the setting for Jesus' early ministry. Here, he often preached to crowds, teaching about the Kingdom of God.

## Galilee

Once he had prepared himself spiritually in the wilderness (*see* page 10) Jesus began his ministry of teaching and healing in and around Galilee. Since Jesus was a Jew it was quite natural that he should preach in synagogues. But he offended many other Jews by claiming to be the Son of God and to be able to forgive people's sins – which, they said, only God had the power to do. They also rejected his claim to be the Messiah. Surely the Messiah, who it was believed would save Israel from its enemies, would be a mighty ruler or warrior – not a humble carpenter's son from Nazareth! When Jesus was forced out of the synagogues he spent much of the time preaching in the open air attracting larger and larger crowds who listened closely to what he had to say.

*a été reçu membre de l'Association de la Ste Enfance le*

*Left* This idealized picture of Jesus blessing children of different nations attempts to show his gentleness and the trust he inspired in young people.

# 'The people brought to Jesus all who had various kinds of sickness, and laying his hands on each one, he healed them.'

Luke 4:40

**Above** *A child herds sheep in the Judaean desert. Jesus' stories, or parables, used images from everyday life – such as the shepherd searching for his lost sheep – to explain God's love for humanity.*

### His message

Jesus called on the people to repent of their sins and to prepare for the coming of the Kingdom of God on Earth. But it was a lot to ask of simple farmers who spent most of their time planting crops in the fields or tending their sheep and goats on the hillsides. So he used a simple language that everyone could understand, using examples from everyday life to make his point. His parables made everyone sit up and think. Yes, they knew how important it was to go after a single lost sheep so, yes, they had an idea of why it was important for God to save the life of one human sinner and bring him or her back to the fold.

### Charisma

The Gospels tell us that Jesus was an immensely popular figure in first-century Palestine. He was a friend to the poor, the needy and the outcasts of society and, in particular, he had a very special relationship with children. He loved their simplicity and directness and said that people should become as trusting as children if they wanted to enter the Kingdom of Heaven.

### Jerusalem

Although traditionally Jesus has been described as 'meek and mild', he also had other important characteristics in the form of strength and natural authority. When he came to Jerusalem for the last time before his crucifixion he was not afraid to challenge the priests and religious authorities of the city directly. He did this with the knowledge that his claim to be the Son of God would lead to rejection and a slow and agonizing death on the cross.

**Above** *Another side of Jesus' character emerges in this modern advertisement which portrays him as a strong and fearless revolutionary leader.*

# THE CRUCIFIXION

The crucifixion of Christ and his resurrection from the dead are at the core of Christian belief. Jesus' anguish as he approached death and his agony on the cross with nails through his hands and feet, as described in the Gospels, have come to be called the Passion.

## The first covenant

The Old Testament Book of Genesis says that God created humans in the form of Adam and Eve and made an earthly paradise known as the Garden of Eden. According to Genesis, which many Christians interpret symbolically, Adam and Eve rebelled and were cast out of paradise – a doctrine known as the Fall. The long process then began to liberate people from sin and to restore God's kingdom on Earth. God's next attempt involved a covenant with Noah. God promised that Noah and his family, and pairs of animals would be spared from a destructive flood by escaping on an ark (vast boat). But after the flood had subsided, humanity returned to its wicked ways and worshipped false idols.

## The second covenant

God's second covenant was with Abraham and the people of Israel, but again the people sinned. Something urgent had to be done once and for all, so God decided to make what Christians believe is the ultimate sacrifice, to free creation from its wickedness: God came to Earth in human form, in Jesus, knowing that he would die on the cross. With this supreme act of self-sacrifice Jesus, the promised Messiah, would save humanity from sin.

With the crucifixion and the resurrection Christians believe that God, through Christ, has ultimately broken the power of the devil and offered salvation to all those who want it.

*Above* In the top section Judas, one of the disciples, betrays Christ with a kiss. He was so ashamed that he later committed suicide. In the bottom section, Jesus is brought before Pilate.

*Left* Christ was made to carry his own cross to Golgotha and he was mocked by the people. In many parts of the world, this scene is re-enacted every Easter.

*Above Jesus was stripped naked, beaten and crowned with thorns as a mocking reminder that he had claimed to be King of the Jews.*

## 'And Jesus cried with a loud voice, and gave up the ghost.'

Mark 15:37

**The story of Christ's Passion**
Jesus' claim to be the Messiah and his criticism of the Temple's empty rituals angered the religious authorities. At one point Jesus went into the Temple compound, overturned the moneychangers' tables and announced that they were turning the house of God into a marketplace. The chief priests feared that Jesus would destroy their authority and decided to have him arrested. They did a deal with one of his disciples, Judas Iscariot. In exchange for 30 pieces of silver, Judas agreed to betray Jesus. Jesus knew this and said so (Mark 14:18–21) at the Last Supper. He went to the Garden of Gethsemane to pray and to ask God to release him from his fate, but finally realized that God's will, not his own, had to be done.

As Jesus was about to leave the Garden of Gethsemane, he and his disciples were surrounded by soldiers. Judas Iscariot stepped forward and kissed Jesus – this was a signal to let the soldiers know whom to arrest. Jesus was tried before Pontius Pilate, the Roman governor, who found him guilty of no crime. However, he agreed to the mob's wishes and had Jesus crucified on a hill called Golgotha (the place of the skull) between two criminals.

After some hours on the cross Jesus died in agony with the words, 'Father, into thy hands I commend my spirit' (Luke 23:46). Immediately there was an earthquake and part of the Temple was destroyed. Three days later the Bible says Jesus rose again from the dead and told his disciples that they should now spread the message of God's love for humankind and the hope of life after death.

# THE TRINITY

Christians traditionally believe that Jesus Christ had a divine father (God) and an earthly mother (Mary). They believe Christ to be both human and divine.

### The Incarnation

The doctrine of the Incarnation (Latin *caro* meaning 'flesh') is summed up in statements at the beginning of John's Gospel: 'In the beginning was the Word, and the Word was with God, and the Word was God ... and the Word was made flesh'. Christians understand the 'Word' to mean the divine plan underlying all Creation, a plan that is not separate from God Himself. The divine plan was revealed to humanity in the flesh and blood of one man, Jesus, who similarly is not separate from God Himself. Jesus is one with God. Father and Son are one.

### The Holy Spirit

After his ascension into Heaven, Jesus was no longer visible in the world, but the Bible says he communicated with humanity through his Holy Spirit, which descended on the disciples at Pentecost. God, Christ and the Holy Spirit are known as the Trinity, or three persons in one God – God the Father, God the Son and God the Holy Spirit – rather than a collection of three gods. This idea has long been debated by Christians and they still fail to agree. A mainstream Christian belief is that the Trinity represents three aspects of God, or three ways in which God exists.

*Above This painting,* The Descent of the Holy Ghost, *is by Sandro Botticelli (c.1441–1510). In Christian doctrine the Trinity – Father, Son and Holy Spirit (or Ghost) – are thought of as three aspects of the one God.*

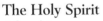

*Left Masai women attend a Pentecostal service in Tanzania. Charismatic or Pentecostal Christians believe that the gifts of the Holy Spirit help them to heal the sick.*

*Above* In Christian imagery God often appears as a wise and powerful old man, a patriarch like Moses. This is how the artist Michelangelo portrayed God's creation of the first man on Earth, Adam.

*Below* The Lamb of God is a powerful symbol of Christian redemption. This picture of the lamb in heaven comes from a manuscript called the Lambeth Apocalypse (c.1260CE).

### Knowing the unknowable

Christians believe that God is infinite and eternal and, as such, beyond human understanding. However, some Christians see the Creator as an all-powerful, or omnipotent, father figure, who cares for humanity as a father cares for his children, loving at all times but also occasionally strict. But other Christians say this description is not sufficient. They point to other imagery in the Bible that stresses the feminine side of God's nature, and even refer to God as 'Our Heavenly Father and Mother'.

### The Lamb of God

Through the second person of the Trinity, Jesus Christ, Christians believe that other aspects of God's nature have been revealed. An image often used is that of the lamb. This has its origins in the Jewish tradition of sacrificing a lamb at Passover, but in Christian thinking it means that God so loved the world that He was prepared to pay the ultimate price – the sacrifice of His only son – to buy back (redeem) the world from the clutches of sin and death.

> **'There is one body and one spirit, one Lord, one faith, one baptism, one God and Father of all.'**
>
> Ephesians IV:4–6

# CHRISTIAN WORSHIP

Christian worship can take place anywhere and at any time, but it is usually carried out privately with prayers in the home, or publicly at church services attended by a congregation or community of believers. Worship takes many different forms. For example, it can be full of ceremony with priests and bishops dressed in colourful robes or vestments; or it can be a simple gathering of Christians meeting together for prayer at someone's house. There may be loud music with trumpets, organs, guitars and choirs, or there may be quiet meditation in the silence of a plain room. Jesus said that all that was needed for Christian worship to begin was the presence of people gathered together in his name.

In practice most Christians consider Sunday a special day to be set aside for worship in church. They meet to say prayers, sing hymns and hear extracts of the Bible. The priest or minister will deliver a sermon, or short talk, designed to explain an aspect of the Christian life. After the service there might be Bible study or Sunday school classes in the church hall.

*Above Christian prayer is essentially a conversation with God. Children are taught that, even though they cannot see him, Jesus is with them always.*

### The five themes

Christian worship focuses on five principal themes – adoration, praise, thanksgiving, repentance and petition. Adoration is the

expression of the love that Christians believe is owed to God the Creator who sacrificed His only son to save the world. Praise is the passionate celebration of God's splendour, power and majesty. Thanksgiving is the expression of gratitude for the gift of life. Repentance involves the confession of sin and the promise to be a better person, and petition is the equally human request for help in times of need.

*Left A young girl lighting candles at a Catholic church service in Lithuania. Candles have always been important in Christian worship as a symbol of the light that Jesus brought into the world.*

## THE LORD'S PRAYER

Our Father who art in Heaven, hallowed be thy name. Thy kingdom come. Thy will be done on Earth as it is in Heaven. Give us this day our daily bread. Forgive us our trespasses as we forgive those who trespass against us. And lead us not into temptation but deliver us from evil. For thine is the kingdom, the power and the glory. For ever and ever. Amen. (Matthew 6:9–13)

*Below Singing hymns is a popular part of a Christian church service. The music is traditionally played on a organ and there is usually a choir to lead the congregation.*

## The Lord's Prayer

The New Testament contains the prayer that Jesus taught his followers to say, the Lord's Prayer. It is central to Christian worship in that it provides a model of prayer and tells believers what Christ himself considered important about relationships with God and with one another. It is sometimes asked why, if God knows all our needs already (Matthew 6:32), there is any requirement to pray at all. There are two answers to this. The first is simple: Christ prayed, so Christians should do so too. The second answer is that God wants us to co-operate with Him, rather than expect Him to do everything for us.

*Above At Holy Communion, the priest or minister blesses the bread and wine and the worshippers receive them in memory of the body and blood of Christ.*

## Church worship

There is a carefully prepared structure to most church worship, which is known as the liturgy. This lays down the form of the prayers, the order of service and the choice of readings. In some traditions (notably the Orthodox), this structure has not changed for generations, and people go to a church service knowing exactly what to expect. In more modern forms of worship (especially within the Evangelical tradition), the whole service seems more informal and spontaneous. Members of the congregation are encouraged to take part – either in the preparation of the liturgy or in the leading of the prayers. In some (nowadays rare) Roman Catholic services the entire service takes place in Latin. But whatever form Christian worship takes, human beings are gathered together in friendship to offer praise and thanks to God.

# THE SACRAMENTS

C hristian worship often focuses on scenes from Christ's earthly ministry and uses them symbolically to mark important turning points in people's lives.

### The sacrament of baptism

The first of these is the sacrament of baptism. A sacrament is defined as 'an outward and visible sign of an inward and spiritual grace'. Baptism marks admission to the Christian Church and recalls the moment, at the beginning of Christ's ministry, when he was baptized by John the Baptist in the waters of the River Jordan. Today, there are two forms of this ritual – infant and adult baptism – and there is debate as to which form is preferable. Some say that admission to the Church should be delayed until people are old enough to make this commitment for themselves. Others argue that people should be welcomed into the community of believers as soon as possible, shortly after birth.

> **'You are all the children of God by faith in Christ Jesus.'**
>
> Galatians III:26–8

In most churches there is a font (ceremonial bowl) or pool set aside for baptism. Baptism with water has its origins in early purification rites, but in Christianity it is used as a visible sign that the child is being born again into a new life in Christ. Normally the mother and father choose godparents, who take part in the ceremony and promise to look after the child's spiritual development.

Adult baptism frequently involves total immersion in the water, which symbolizes purification from the sins of Adam and Eve and the beginning of a new life in obedience to Christ. The minister and helpers stand waist deep in the water and, after prayers, tip the person backwards and totally immerse him or her for a second or two.

*Above* In some traditions, baptism is considered such an important rite of passage that only those who have made a mature decision to become a Christian may be baptized – usually by total immersion in the water.

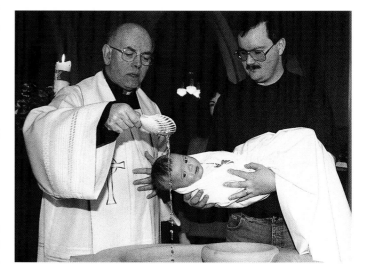

*Right* Children are baptized by a priest or minister, who welcomes them into the Christian Church by pouring water over their foreheads.

## The Eucharist

Known as holy communion, the Lord's Supper, the Mass, and the Divine Liturgy, the Eucharist commemorates the Last Supper when Jesus told his disciples to take bread and wine in remembrance of his body and blood. Worshippers receive a small piece of bread or a wafer and a sip of wine or juice to symbolize this. Roman Catholics believe that these become the actual body and blood of Christ.

*Above* A marriage in church is both a joyful event and a solemn exchange of vows. Here, an Orthodox Christian wedding takes place in Sofia, Bulgaria.

## Confirmation

Protestants generally acknowledge two sacraments (baptism and the Eucharist) while Catholics and Orthodox recognise seven and include confirmation, holy matrimony, penance, ordination and the anointing of the dying. People who have been baptized as infants often want to renew their commitment to the faith as adults. They do this by confirmation which takes place after instruction by a priest or minister. In Protestant and Catholic churches the confirmation is usually carried out by a bishop who lays hands on the person's head to signify that Christ's living spirit is being passed on. They then become full members of the church and may receive Holy Communion.

*Below* Full members of the church take holy communion in remembrance of the Last Supper. Here, Mass is being celebrated in Zimbabwe.

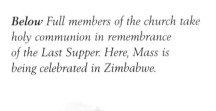

## Holy matrimony

During the sacrament of holy matrimony the bride and groom vow to remain faithful to each other until death. Marriages call to mind Jesus' miracle at the wedding feast in Cana, where he turned water into wine (*see* page 11). Marriage is also a symbol of Christ's union with his church.

21

# CHRISTMAS

Christmas is the time when Christians remember and celebrate the birth of Jesus Christ. It is a happy time when people give presents in memory of the joy God brought to the world in the form of His only son.

### 'Lighten our darkness'

In the early days of Christianity, Easter was *the* central Christian festival and it was not until 400 years after the birth of Christ that Christmas became an official Christian observance. Before that time there where many folk or pagan midwinter festivals, when people celebrated the fact that the worst of winter was over and that warmer weather was not far away. The early Church modified these existing festivals for its own purpose and gave them a Christian significance. They became an opportunity to celebrate the birth of Christ as 'the Light of the World'.

### Preparing for Christmas

Preparations begin four Sundays before Christmas Day at the start of Advent, which means 'coming'. During this time Christians think about what the arrival of Christ means to them personally as well as to the whole human race. Children are often given an Advent Calendar so they can count down to Christmas Day.

**Above** *Many artists have portrayed Christ as a light coming into the darkness of the world. This painting, entitled* The Light of the World, *is by William Holman Hunt (1827–1910).*

### THE NATIVITY

Only two of the New Testament Gospels, Matthew and Luke, tell the story of Christ's birth, or Nativity. The stories are not the same, but some of the details overlap. The traditional picture that Christians have is a mixture of the two accounts. The baby Jesus was born in a manger, or feeding trough, in a stable surrounded by farm animals. His parents, Mary and Joseph, had been turned away from the inn where they intended to stay because there was no room for them. To mark the event, Three Wise Men, or Magi, were guided by a star to the manger. They laid gifts of gold, frankincense and myrrh at the infant's feet. Children frequently re-enact the scene in school Nativity plays.

*Above* The presents brought by the Magi are symbolic. The gold suggests Christ's majesty as a king and Messiah. Frankincense and myrrh are sweet-smelling resins from the bark of certain trees. They also have healing properties, which make them useful for embalming (preserving) dead bodies.

# 'Magi came from the East to Jerusalem and asked, "Where is the one who has been born King of the Jews?"'

(Matthew 2:1-2)

In most Christian traditions Christmas Day is celebrated on December 25 – though the Orthodox Christmas is on January 6. Homes are decorated with holly and ivy, plants that symbolize Christ's eternal presence in the world. Christmas carols that tell of Christ's birth are sung, and in many churches Mass is held at midnight on Christmas Eve so that worshippers can enter into the joy of Christmas from the beginning of Christmas Day.

Christmas in the West has become very commercialized, but even some of the secular elements have religious roots. Father Christmas, or Santa Claus, is based on the patron saint of children, St Nicholas, who is traditionally associated with the giving of presents. Despite the pressure to spend money and to 'eat, drink and be merry', many people still catch a glimpse of the pure joy that Christ's birth is believed to have brought to the world.

## The Three Wise Men

The Festival of Epiphany in early January celebrates the arrival of the Three Wise Men, who were the first gentiles (non-Jews) to see Christ. This shows that Christ's message – peace on Earth and goodwill to all humanity – is a universal one and that salvation is open to anyone who believes in Him.

# CELEBRATING EASTER

The Easter season is the most important time of year for Christian believers and a time of both sadness and joy. On Good Friday they remember the Crucifixion when Jesus Christ was put to death on the cross. On Easter Sunday, they remember the Resurrection – the day he rose from the dead.

The 40 days before Easter is a special time for Christian prayer and contemplation. The period is known as Lent and people deny themselves pleasures such as sweets. The story of Easter is told in the New Testament. Jesus claimed to be the Son of God and was considered a threat by the Jewish and Roman authorities. On Good Friday, he was crucified on a hill outside Jerusalem on the order of Pontius Pilate. Later that day, his followers took his body and buried it in a tomb – a cave sealed with a stone. On the third day, celebrated now as Easter Sunday, women followers went to visit the tomb. They discovered that the stone had been rolled away. The body of Jesus had gone and in its place were two angels who said, 'Why do you look for the living among the dead? He is not here, but has risen'.

*Above* In many faiths, the egg is a symbol of life. This Easter egg, studded with jewels, was made for the Russian tsar Nicholas II.

*Above* Jesus Christ rises from the dead and steps out of the tomb on Easter Day. Although this Italian painting is more than 500 years old, the scene is still central to Christian belief.

*Right* On the night before Easter every year, Christians at the Church of the Holy Sepulchre in Jerusalem celebrate the ceremony of 'new light' with candles. The church is a blaze of light as flares are passed from hand to hand.

*Above* Fish symbols, often associated with Christ, decorate this Ukrainian Easter egg.

> '**Fear not … I know that you seek Jesus who was crucified. He is not here. For he has risen …'**
>
> Matthew 28:5–6

To mark the joy of this event, Christians break their Lenten fast on Easter Sunday and celebrate with a feast. Holy Week and Easter have always been celebrated by Christians as a time to remember that God loves people so much that He sent His son, Jesus, to die for the world. As a result, Easter has always been a special time for the baptism of new Christians.

Even before Christian times, many people celebrated spring in a special way. It is the season when trees sprout leaves again, when nature is 'reborn' after the deadness of winter – just as Jesus rose from the dead. People held spring festivals, and many of their traditions carried over into the Christian Easter. The giving of Easter eggs, for example, goes back to pre-Christian times. The egg, from which a chick will be born, is a sign of fertility, a reminder that older generations die but younger ones will eventually take their place.

### THE HISTORY OF EASTER BREAD

Special cakes are eaten at Easter. The hot cross bun (below left) bears the sign of the cross on which Jesus was crucified. The fruit and spices that are used to make the bun are a reminder of the happiness that his resurrection brings. For centuries, the people living in Frankfurt, Germany, ate pretzels (far right) at their very popular Easter fairs.

# THE RELIGIOUS LIFE

In every religion there are individuals who feel drawn to a more intense form of spiritual experience. As a result some may feel a vocation (calling) to religious life and to an extra degree of Christian commitment.

### The ordained ministry

To become priests or ministers, candidates have to persuade the Church that their commitment is genuine and that they are intellectually and temperamentally suited for ordination. In the Roman Catholic and Orthodox traditions only men can become priests. After selection they undergo several years of training, during which time they learn about the history and traditions of the Church, study the Bible and other books of Christian theology, and learn about the practical requirements of being a Christian leader. Once they have been ordained, they may be given a parish (a geographical area with its own church) where they will look after people's needs.

### Monks and nuns

Some people feel called to take up the religious life as monks or nuns in monasteries or convents. They take three vows – of poverty, chastity and obedience – and live a very disciplined life, deliberately set apart from the outside world. There are many religious groups, or orders. Among the best known are the Dominicans, the Franciscans, the Benedictines, the Carmelites, the Cistercians and the Trappists. Some of these are enclosed, contemplative orders in which monks and nuns devote themselves to prayer and reflection in a community that is completely cut off from the outside world. Other orders have considerable contact with the world and work with people who need their help.

*Above* St Francis lived a life of self-denial and was said to be very close to nature. Birds and animals felt safe in his presence and it is even said that they came to hear him preach.

*Right* Pilgrims were a familiar sight on the roads of Europe in the 15th century. Here, they are making their way to the cathedral at Santiago de Compostela in northern Spain.

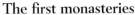

## The first monasteries

The pattern of western monasticism was set by an Italian, St Benedict (*c.*480–550CE). At the age of 14, he became a hermit and his devotion to Christ's austere way of life attracted many followers. In the mid-6th century he established a monastery at Monte Casino, between Rome and Naples, and drew up what is known as the Rule of St Benedict. This involves a strict timetable of study, prayer and manual work within the community, which is headed by an abbot. During the Middle Ages the monasteries became great centres of learning and they preserved many ancient manuscripts.

## Saints and martyrs

Perhaps the most popular saint of all is St Francis (*c.*1181– 1226CE), who was born into a rich Italian family but renounced his wealth when he felt God calling him to a life of service. One night while he was praying, an angel is said to have appeared to him and given him the *stigmata* – wounds to his hands, feet and side in imitation of Christ's wounds on the cross.

Over the years many men and women have been persecuted for their faith and martyred for it. The first Christian martyr was St Stephen, who was charged with blasphemy (speaking disrespectfully about God) by the Jewish authorities and stoned to death in Jerusalem in about 35CE. Many martyrs became holy figures venerated by the Church. St Catherine of Alexandria was a 4th-century saint and martyr who opposed Roman persecution and was strapped to a spiked wheel and tortured to death. The Catherine wheel has given its name to a firework that spins round when lit. The Roman Catholic Church uses a process known as 'canonization' to declare someone a saint and requires evidence of great devotion and some sort of miraculous event associated with their life. However, numerous men and women who have led saintly lives have not been officially declared saints.

**Above** *Religious men and women are not always confined to monasteries and convents. Here, an African nun helps care for sick children at a medical mission.*

# CATHEDRALS AND CHURCHES

The earliest followers of Jesus met anywhere they could to worship God – in fields, in cellars, in other people's homes – but as time went by and they increased in confidence and numbers, they wanted to create special places set aside for worship.

## Churches

The Christian churches that have been built over the centuries reflect a variety of architectural styles but they have a number of basic symbols in common. For example, many are built in the shape of a cross to represent Christ's crucifixion. And the sanctuary, containing the altar or Holy Table, is often situated at the end of the building which faces Jerusalem – the city where Christians believe Christ rose from the dead.

*Below Chartres Cathedral in northern France represents one of Europe's finest examples of medieval cathedral building.*

## Cathedrals

The medieval period, between *c.*1100 and *c.*1500CE, saw a huge growth in church building in Europe. The result was the construction of the most magnificent cathedrals people had ever seen, expressing both the power and the influence of Christianity in the world. A cathedral takes its name from the Greek word meaning 'seat' and is a large church where a bishop symbolically sets down his seat of authority within the diocese or area under his control. To this day cathedrals are associated with the best in art and architecture and are places where the finest music can be heard.

*Right In this aerial view of St Andrew's Cathedral, Singapore, the 'cruciform' or cross-like shape of a Christian Church is clearly visible. The dramatic spires are other significant architectural symbols pointing heavenwards up to God.*

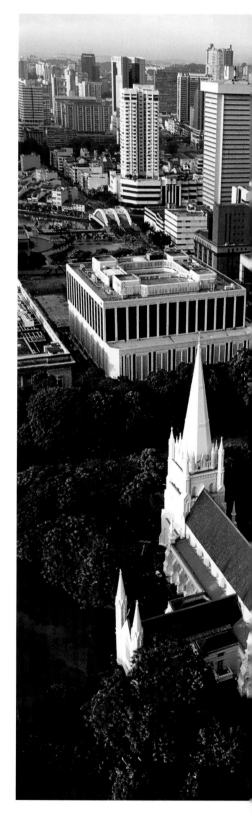

### House Churches

Many Christians nowadays look to the example of the early Church and see no need for a special building. They may meet in an old cinema, for example, or a school hall where they can sing and pray without having to worry about maintaining an expensive structure. A growing number of people who belong to the House Church Movement prefer to meet in each other's homes to express their faith in God.

***Above*** *The House Church Movement believes that people rather than buildings are the foundation of the Christian Church. Here, a group of Christians worship in the informal setting of a private home.*

### Social centres

Churches also provide a social centre where believers can meet in friendship not only to worship but to talk, to laugh, to have meals together and to organize events for the whole community. Churches are also places where Christian faith expresses itself in active concern for others. Some churches may run clubs and activities for the young and the elderly, or provide crèches and nursery care for young children. Other churches, particularly in inner city areas, distribute food to the hungry and organize shelter for the homeless.

***Below*** *The church also functions as a social centre. At this American church in Washington DC free meals are handed out to the homeless.*

# MISSIONARIES

The early Christians were told to spread the good news of Christ throughout the world and to take the message of salvation to every corner of the Earth. Paul (*see* page 8) took the Gospel throughout the eastern Mediterranean to Rome. Others after him took the same message as far afield as Persia and India. In the 16th century CE, the Roman Catholic Church began to export the Christian faith to Mexico, South America, and Africa, and then to China and Japan.

### The purpose of mission

The first large-scale missions were led by the Spanish and the Portuguese. They were often so associated with trade and territorial expansion that the Christian message was frequently confused with conquest and control. In fact, the early Spanish adventurers were known as the *Conquistadors* or conquerors, and the religion that came with them sometimes seemed as unfriendly as their swords and guns.

The early missionaries expected the indigenous, or native, people to behave as Europeans, imposing ways of dressing or eating that were inappropriate for the men and women of South America, India or Japan. Later missionaries learned the importance of working with the local culture and of accepting the way of life of those they were trying to serve and help.

*Above* The Jesuits have long been associated with missionary work around the world. Here, a missionary helps to look after the welfare and education of children on the Puluwat Islands of Micronesia.

*Left* Missionary work involves practical help as well as spiritual teaching. Food aid to countries in need is part of that process. Here, grain is stored for distribution among those affected by drought or famine.

*Above* The traffic in missionary work is not one way. Here, a nun from Africa helps a European priest to administer Holy Communion to his congregation.

## Service

Throughout its long history, Christian mission has sometimes been associated with power and domination. But that is only part of the story. Equally, many Christian men and women have given up everything to travel to remote and dangerous places to tell other people about an experience that has changed their lives.

They have also brought a strong sense of service, helping to build schools and hospitals, bringing food and medicines, and supporting communities that are less well-off than those in richer, developed countries. Although they are sometimes accused of using their wealth to persuade local people to convert to Christianity, most modern missionaries offer their help with no conditions attached. Instead, they let their work speak for itself.

*Above* A Japanese print showing Portuguese Catholic missionaries bringing the message of the Christian Gospels to Japan in the late 16th century CE.

## Two-way traffic

One of the aims of mission is to help people build up local communities and churches and to train the next generation of leaders to run the churches for themselves. In turn, many of these churches send out their own missionaries to other countries. The West, they argue, has forgotten what real Christianity is all about and has put its faith in money and success. So missionaries from Africa, for example, come to Europe to spread the Christian message and show that mission does not flow in only one direction.

# DIVISIONS IN CHRISTIANITY

Many Christians find it sad that the community that Jesus Christ founded as a unified family of believers is deeply divided. Divisions emerged shortly after Christ's death, when early Christians disagreed over the exact detail of his teaching and how it should be put into practice. The first major split, or schism, was in 1054CE, when the Church divided into two branches – Eastern and Western.

*Above The traditions of the eastern Orthodox Church have remained unchanged for centuries.*

### The Eastern or Orthodox tradition
This grew out of the Byzantine Empire (the eastern part of the Roman Empire) of which Constantinople became the capital in 476CE. Its influence spread to Greece, central Europe and Russia, and the most important groups today are the Russian, Greek, Armenian, Serbian and Romanian Orthodox Churches that put great emphasis on tradition.

### The Western or Roman Catholic tradition
The western tradition produced a Church based on the authority of the Bishop of Rome, who is in direct succession to the apostle Simon (later called Peter). The Pope is held by some to be infallible – in other words, his opinion on theological matters cannot be wrong and must be followed by Roman Catholics everywhere. The refusal by the Orthodox Church to accept papal authority was one of the reasons for the Great Schism. Roman Catholics are the largest group of Christians today, with around 890 million adherents. Outside Europe, South America has most Roman Catholics.

*Below Barbara Harris was the first female bishop of the Episcopal Church of the United States. The role of women in the ordained ministry of the Christian Church is a source of deep theological division.*

*Above* Evangelical or Charismatic worship is informal and spontaneous. These people are praying at a religious service at Newport Beach, California.

*Below* Pope John Paul II gives First Communion to Roman Catholic children in Trondheim, Norway. The Pope is the head of the Roman Catholic Church.

## The Protestants

The Reformation began in the 14th century when people like Jan Hus, a preacher in Prague, attacked the Roman Catholic Church for its excessive wealth and its departure from the simple teaching of Christ. But most people date the Reformation from 1517, when the German theologian Martin Luther nailed 95 criticisms ('theses') of the Church to the door of the cathedral in Wittenberg. He argued that people did not need priests and the Pope to mediate between themselves and God. He stressed a personal relationship with Christ and a close study of the Bible as a way towards salvation. His followers – who protested – became known as Protestants.

## Many denominations

Despite internal tensions the Roman Catholic Church continues to be a unified body, but Protestantism has fragmented into many different denominations – Anglicanism, Lutheranism, Methodism, Presbyterianism and many others that share the core beliefs about Jesus Christ and his ministry but worship in different ways. A modern phenomenon in the West is the so-called House Church Movement (*see* page 29), which has abandoned the traditional institutions of the Church and worships in an informal style. Members tend to belong to the Evangelical or Charismatic wing of Christianity, that is to say, they put great emphasis on the gifts of the spirit and on a personal encounter with Jesus Christ. There are some theological disagreements between the liberal wing of the Church and those Evangelicals who interpret the Bible in a more literal way, but all Christians are trying to wrestle with the challenges contained in the Gospel and to make the faith a living reality in their lives.

# THE CHURCH IN THE TWENTY-FIRST CENTURY

The Christian Church is a collection of people from across the world (and throughout time). Although Christians come from many different cultures, they are united in Jesus' name to serve and worship God. But that does not mean that Christians have always seen eye to eye. Far from it. Being human and imperfect, Christians have frequently disagreed with each other, both in the past and in the present, about what is expected of them and about how they should behave in the world. Even when they look to scripture for guidance Christians do not always agree – the Bible cannot be used by people as a simple rule book.

## Reading the Bible

Christians believe that the Bible contains the 'Word of God' but there is often debate about what that phrase actually means. Some Christians believe that the Bible has to be read literally as if every word had been 'dictated' by God alone. They see no errors, contradictions or ambiguities.

Others, however, say that certain passages have to be read not as literal fact but closer to poetry – as an unfolding story (twists, turns, contradictions and all) of God's purpose for human beings. The words, therefore, have to be interpreted wisely. Christians also argue that the Bible is a product of the time when it was written and that it says certain things about slaves, for example, or women, or Jews, that are no longer true. In this way, the Bible has to be constantly reinterpreted in the light of what we know today about the world.

*Above* *For more than 2,000 years, the Bible has spoken directly to people of all backgrounds. This young boy studies his Bible in English and, according to Christians, comes face to face with the divinely inspired Word of God.*

*Right* Christ Glorified in the Court of Heaven *by the Italian painter, Fra Angelico (c.1400-1455CE). This imaginary portrayal of Christ amid the splendour of Paradise is one artist's way of showing the joy that Christians believe awaits all those who have put their faith in Jesus Christ, the Saviour.*

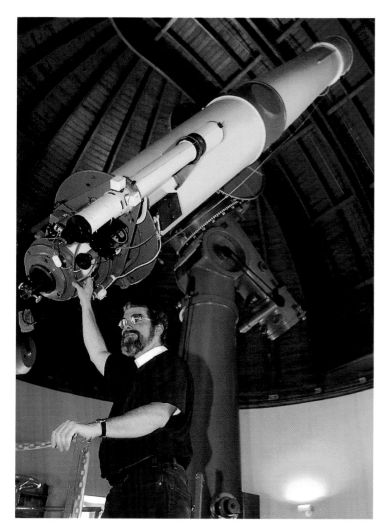

*Above A Catholic astronomer at the Vatican's observatory in Castelgandolfo, outside Rome, prepares to survey the night sky in order to learn more about the universe. Most Christians see no conflict between their faith and science.*

*Right A mother-to-be is examined by ultrasound. An image of her unborn child is visible on the monitor. Such technology was unheard of at the time of Christ but Christians today can apply his teachings to new questions thrown up by technological advances.*

## The challenges of the modern world

Advances in science, technology and medicine and the rapid pace of social change over the last 150 years have thrown up new challenges for today's Christians. Organ transplants, life support machines, space exploration, fertility treatments and so on did not exist when the Bible was originally written. In a similar way, ethical questions such as sexual morality, abortion, artificial contraception, the care of the natural environment and the treatment of animals continue to divide Christian opinion. The challenge is to apply the teachings of Jesus to every new situation that arises.

## A radical solution

The radical solution Jesus proposed was as much a challenge to his followers 2,000 years ago as it is to Christians today and in any age. He told them to prepare for the Kingdom of God. In doing so, they would be enacting God's love for the world and at the same time paving the way for Christ's ultimate return when, as God has decreed from the beginning of time, all pain, suffering and death would vanish forever.

Christians believe that life on Earth is part of a much bigger picture. For them, physical death is not an end but a beginning. Their hope is that by treating one's neighbour as oneself, by leading a godly life, by trusting in the living person of Jesus Christ and by listening to the inner voice of the Holy Spirit they can ultimately achieve everlasting life in the company of God. And, even more importantly, that this is possible not just for all Christians but for the whole of humankind.

# GLOSSARY

**Advent** The four week period of spiritual preparation before Christmas.

**Anoint** To apply oil to a person as part of a religious ceremony to appoint a priest or a king.

**Apostle** One of the 12 chief disciples of Jesus.

**Baptism** The ritual of admission to the Christian Church – involving sprinkling with or immersion in water.

**Blasphemy** Insulting talk that is made about God.

**Charismatic** Inspirational. Also possessing the gifts of the Holy Spirit, for example healing and speaking in tongues.

**Church** A building for Christian worship. Also, the body of Christian believers.

**Communion** Being with and sharing something.

**Congregation** Those attending a church service.

**Covenant** An agreement or contract.

**Convent** A religious community of women (nuns).

**Crucifixion** A form of execution frequently used by the Romans whereby those condemned to death were fixed to a wooden cross and left to die.

**Divine** Of or from God.

**Epistle** A letter.

**Eucharist** The sharing of bread and wine in remembrance of the Last Supper.

**Everlasting life** Eternal life with God after physical death on Earth.

**Fast** Abstaining from food as part of a spiritual discipline.

**Forgiveness** The act of pardoning someone for wrongs that have been done.

**Good Friday** The day commemorating the Crucifixion and death of Christ.

**Gospel** The record of Christ's life and his teaching contained in the first four books of the New Testament of the Bible.

**Holy Communion** The sharing of bread and wine in memory of the Last Supper (*see also* Eucharist).

**Holy Spirit** The third person of the Christian Trinity and God's unseen spiritual energy at work in the world. Also known as the Holy Ghost.

**House Church** Groups of Christians meeting in private homes to worship God.

**Icon** A religious painting used as an aid to devotion and prayer.

**Incarnation** The Christian doctrine stating that God became a human being in the form of Jesus Christ.

**Kingdom of God** A perfect society in accordance with God's divine plan.

**Lamb of God** Jesus, the ultimate sacrifice made by God to save the world from sin.

**Lent** The period of self-denial and reflection commemorating Jesus' 40 days in the wilderness.

**Liturgy** Forms of worship.

**Lord's Prayer** The 'Our Father' prayer that was taught to the 12 disciples by Jesus.

**Martyr** Someone who is prepared to suffer or die for their faith.

**Messiah** The 'anointed one' in Hebrew. The saviour of the Jewish nation foretold in the Old Testament and believed by Christians to be Jesus, the saviour of the whole world. 'Christ' comes from the Greek word for 'anointed one'.

**Miracle** A supernatural event signifying God's action. Jesus performed many miracles.

**Mission** Christian work involving the spreading of the good news of Christ.

**Missionary** A person spreading the message of Christ and doing good work in God's name.

**Monastery** A religious community of men (monks).

**Nativity** The birth of Christ, as told in Matthew and Luke.

**New Testament** The second section of the Christian Bible beginning with the appearance of Jesus Christ on Earth.

**Old Testament** The Hebrew Bible explaining the origin and purpose of life under God.

**Ordain** To make someone a priest.

**Parable** A story using simple language to convey a spiritual message.

**Passion** The final hours of Jesus Christ's life on Earth from the Last Supper to the Crucifixion.

**Pentecost** The moment when the Holy Spirit descended on the disciples and filled them with God's power.

**Pilgrim** A person who travels to a sacred place for spiritual reasons.

**Pilgrimage** A journey to a sacred place.

**Pope** The head of the Roman Catholic Church.

**Priest** An ordained member of the Church.

**Redeem** To buy back, especially to pay the price for human sin.

**Repentance** The act of turning away from sin and resolving to lead a good life.

**Resurrection** Jesus' rising from the dead.

**Sacrament** A religious ceremony representing the visible sign of inner spiritual activity.

**Sacrifice** Offering something precious for the sake of God.

**Saint** A holy and devout person who is particularly strong in his or her faith.

**Salvation** The act of saving from sin and death.

**Schism** A split in the church.

**Scripture** Sacred writings.

**Sect** A small group of people believing different things than the mainstream of believers.

**Sin** An action deliberately contrary to God's will.

**Theologian** A person who studies religious thought.

**Trinity** The doctrine stating that in God there are three persons, Father, Son and Holy Spirit, who are believed by Christians to make up God.

**Worship** A ceremony or ceremonies in honour of God.

# INDEX

# ACKNOWLEDGEMENTS

The Publisher would like to thank the following for permission to reproduce their material. Every care has been taken to trace copyright holders. However, if there have been unintentional omissions or failure to trace copyright holders, we apologise and will, if informed, endeavour to make corrections in any future edition.

Cover main and inset Corbis; page 1 Getty Imagebank; 6 Bridgeman Art Library/Giraudon/Louvre, Paris; 7tl Hutchison Library; 7bl Magnum Photos/Stuart Franklin; 8tr Tim Slade; 8b E.T.Archive/Bibliotheque de l'Arsenal, Paris; 9tr Michael Holford; 9bl Bridgeman Art Library/ Bibliotheque Nationale, Paris; 10tr Tate Gallery; 10b Bridgeman Art Library/ National Gallery, London; 11tl Bridgeman Art Library/Kunsthistorisches Museum, Vienna; 12bl Mary Evans Picture Library; 12–13t Corbis; Churches Advertising Network; 13tr Panos Pictures; 14tr Bridgeman Art Library/Musee Conde, Chantilly; 14bc Sygma/E. Pasquier; 15tl E.T. Archive/ National Gallery, London; 16bl Trip/D. Butcher; 16tr/Bridgeman Art Library/ Birmingham Museum and Art Gallery; 17t Robert Harding/Roy Rainford; 17bl Bridgeman Art Library/ Lambeth Palace Library; 18tr Robert Harding; 18bl Trip/A. Tjagny-Rjadno; 19tr Collections/ Geoff Howard; 19 bl Sonia Halliday; 20br Robert Harding; 20—21 Robert Harding/E. Simanor; Hutchison Library/Lesley McIntyre; 21tr Hutchison Library/Melanie Friend; 22bl John Walmsley; 22tr Bridgeman Art Library/Keble College, Oxford; 23tl Bridgeman Art Library/Prado, Madrid; 24cl Bridgeman Art Library/Pinacoteca, Sansepolcro; 24tr Bridgeman Art Library; 24bc Magnum/Fred Mayer; 24–25 Altamont Press Inc. USA; 25bc Roy Williams; 26tr Bridgeman Art Library/ San Francesco, Assisi; 26–27 Robin Carter/Wildlife Art; 27br Hutchison Library/Lesley McIntyre; 28bl Alamy; 28–29 Corbis; 29tr Andes Press Agency; 29br Corbis; 30b Still Pictures; 30–31t Getty; 31bl Art Archive; 31tr Andes Press Agency; 32bc Sygma/Ira Wyman; 32tr Sygma; 33tl Trip/S. Grant; 33bl Topham Picturepoint; 34tr Getty; 34b Bridgeman Art Library; 35tl Associated Press; 35br Alamy